Leaning Against the Sun

P O E M S · B Y

Gerald Barrax

THE UNIVERSITY OF ARKANSAS PRESS
Fayetteville
1992

PS
3552
.A732
L43
1992

Copyright © 1992 by Gerald Barrax
All rights reserved
Manufactured in the United States of America

96 95 94 93 92   5 4 3 2 1

The paper used in this publication meets the minimum requirements of the American National Standard for Permanence of Paper for Printed Library Materials Z39.48-1984. ∞

Library of Congress Cataloging-in-Publication Data

Barrax, Gerald W.
    Leaning against the sun: poems / by Gerald Barrax.
        p. cm. ISBN 1-55728-226-9 (c). --ISBN 1-55728-227-7 (p)
    I. Title.
    PS3552.A732L43 1992
    811'.54--dc20   91-12988
                                                                                 CIP

Acknowledgments

A number of poems in this book originally appeared (or will appear) in the following publications, some in slightly different forms:

Black American Literature Forum: "Optimum Distance," "Whose Children Are These?"

Callaloo: "Haunted House," "Not Often Near Such Water," "Polar's TV Fantasy," "Strangers Like Us: Pittsburgh, Raleigh, 1945–1985," "Uniforms," "Universe"

Deep Rivers, A Portfolio: Twenty Contemporary Black American Poets: "She caught a butterfly"

Hayden's Ferry Review: "Eagle. Tiger. Whale."

Loblolly: "Yardwork"

New Virginia Review: "Cello Poem"

Leaning Against the Sun

For my brother, Harold

*The most gentle man I know,
and the best uncle in the world.
He has enriched the lives
of all those who love him.*

Contents

Eagle. Tiger. Whale. • 3

Not Often Near Such Water • 5

Domestic Tranquility • 9

Whose Children Are These? • 10

Special Bus • 12

Strangers Like Us: Pittsburgh,
Raleigh, 1945–1985 • 13

Haunted House • 14

Yardwork • 17

What More? • 20

Plot • 22

Theology • 23

Epigraphs • 24

Greyhound • 29

Polar's TV Fantasy • 30

Sportsfan • 32

War Film: Dying Forever • 34

Uniforms • 36

Where It Came From • 38

Optimum Distance • 44

Universe • 47

Bill Two • 49

Adagio • 51

"She caught a butterfly" • 52

Cello Poem • 53

Leaning Against the Sun

Eagle. Tiger. Whale.

I'm old enough to stand,
a boy looking at himself
in the long mirror of a chifforobe,
Black child with sandy hair
tightly curled, hazel eyes.
I haven't learned the words,
I photograph everything into my cells:
my little yellow dress with puffed pleated shoulders
and my little pearl buttons;
my little high-topped white shoes and yellow socks;
my little blue ribbon somewhere.
The room behind me is dark,
nothing in the mirror but me
as in a spotlight, yet I feel her presence,
my seventeen-year-old mother, beautiful,
leaning somewhere behind me.
    No one can explain what I've seen, a slim Black woman lying on her back, red geyser pumping from her open mouth, she stares into the ceiling's yellow eye. I see her from her right, the foot of the brass bed, my head three feet high. Someone screams "Lord God Lord God he done shot the woman" while the soft splash, splash. I stand so calm, seeing, until somebody yells "Git that chile outta here." Who knows who knows how I got there from next door, visiting Aunt Annie over in Gadsden, for neither mother nor father is there to tell me "Forget it."

                                      dont tell dont
tell James Albert's sister whispers in the dim coal shed.
She has hair everywhere,
the only subject, verb, object, adverb
I can put together.
It's my birthday, I come to her yard
to pick figs from their tree. James Albert's
daddy said I can, I pull a fig,
she whispers "don't tell, don't tell,"
I feel my hand disappear into the hot full-noon mouth
of Alabama's summer solstice,
lips, lips, tongue curling around, probing
the fruit from my paralyzed fist.
She changes my hands from left to right,
leaves me partially ambidextrous and stuttering
to describe it.
                Now that I've read a lot,
I've learned boxes of "reflection," "homicide," "initiation"
to put visions into,
just as we have done with *eagle tiger whale god*
with handles and edges to finger,
inert and seamless,
no desire to break in, not letting anything out.
But there is that boy who can still do this:
In the Zaire rain forest a snow leopard like a ghost leaps
and with its perfect knives
slices open this box I've made.

Not Often Near Such Water

I always swim parallel to shore,
No farther out than where I lose the bottom.
My family watches me, admiring, envious, uneasy.
My island-born wife who never learned to swim,
Our two daughters who are fish in the pools in Raleigh,
Here are unable to get past the first breaker.
Surf City it is. As early as the third day
We hear about and decide on the Outer Banks
Next time.
        I buy a Styrofoam surf board
Because I thought Dara had broken the one
That belonged to the kids in the next beach house.
She hadn't, so the mother refuses our offer to replace it.
I take Shani and the board out to where I can stand
And try to help her ride
One wave in. She does her best,
But soon will have no more of the Atlantic.
        We play Monopoly, collect shells, the girls afraid of crabs.
When we walk the beach on a dark, windy evening,
I am on point, scanning the sand before us
For anything that scuttles.
I like the way waves slant in to the beach
In high wind and storm.
Someone is flying kites
Strung above the water
A long line of black sea birds.
A Marine chopper from Lejeune flies along the shore,

Its heavy growl drowning the surf's frothy rumble.
I daydream Hollywood's World War II LSTs
Hovering out there on the waves.
From the screened porch we watch mast lights, early morning boats
Belling through the mist, nets dipping side to side
For the flounder, snapper, blues, and king mackerel
That we drive to the piers in the afternoons to buy.
    If only one of us swims,
He ought to make a show of benefitting from it.
Twice a day I swim and sun,
Enhancing my indifferent tan
Of African, Indian, and Dutch ancestry.
I lie on the five-foot, coffin-shaped board
And paddle out to ride back in
The way I've seen the big kids do—
Out toward the inconceivable.
I crossed the Pacific in 1955
On the *USNS Sultan* to Clark Air Force Base.
Sea sickness is worse than death.
For two days I was worse than dead.
Then I'm given my shipboard duty for the week:
To go into a little room stacked with records
And play the likes of Les Brown, Ray Anthony,
The DeMarco Sisters, The Four Freshman
Over the military Muzak system.
Out of hundreds of troops peeling potatoes,
Scrubbing pots, associating with food, God chose me away from it.
I have time for the deck, time to be blinded
By what the water does to the sun,
What the water does to the moon
Makes Turner seascapes come to life.

We steam past Bataan, Corregidor,
Shrouded in history on the port and starboard horizons.
In Manila Bay, ships caught and sunk
Still show rusted hulls above the water.
I'd seen war movies enough for self-conscious patriotism,
The curious reverence one feels before memorials of death.
      Water particles don't move along a wave.
They move in circles as the wave passes by.
I'm a landlocked foreign body propelling myself
Against the disturbance that causes the wave phenomenon.
I've been carried away so quietly,
Up and down the swells so easily.
I look back and see far back
Wife and daughters and beach friends
Standing together, a little gathering
Looking out my way.
I hear almost no sound.
Quietly, quietly I will myself to match the ocean's ease
And abandon the surfboard. To swim back to that small crowd.
The ocean seems to be holding its breath too,
Deciding.
I see that I'm not afraid.
The day FDR died they played the "Meditation" from *Thais*
All day on the radio.
I was twelve. I'd already begun violin lessons.
I'm frozen in an attitude between the (I'll make up a name)
Elm tree in the front yard
And cobblestoned Stranahan Street in Pittsburgh.
I've remained in that spot for forty years,
As though that's where I was the moment they announced his death
And began playing his favorite piece all day.
I've learned it, practiced, memorized,

Play it on Youth Day in Warren Methodist Church
When I'm (I'll make this up) about fifteen.
Each time I played it, hear it, I remember him.
There is nothing but fear itself.
    Can they *see* me?
If they knew how *calm* I am!
I'm out here in the first place and swimming so quietly back
Because I thought I was going to drown
In the pool on Washington Boulevard.
Some dissembling boys got me to jump in the deep .
I was ten or eleven and not long up from Alabama,
Had never been near such water. They pulled me out,
Laughing like bad boys, but not before I had memorized
    drowning.
I went to the other end and started learning to swim.
That was damned smart for a kid, instinctively right.

It's Joan, Shani, and Dara that I'm swimming for.
Where was it, before the ships came?
Sierra Leone, Ghana, a dozen places,
Like Kunta Kinte or Gustavas Vassa
Taken from the forest and village to the coast.
But I was older, with two wives and five children.
Oh, the ships. The ships. We are dying, dying there still.
The sea is a choice,
I swim past sharks to the children.
I'm too old for them to lose their father.
    Uneasy, admiring, they see how calm I am, how far I've
    come.
This time, we will all go deeper into the forest.

Domestic Tranquility

I need a ritual to perform,
clean and sane, for this perfect washday,
the sun burning the top of my head
and forearms raised to the line,
the surrogate wind breathing
my wife's blouses, my daughters' dresses and jeans.
I need a formula to recite
free of mumbo jumbo and cant,
as fit for me and this day, and I say
to hell with Kenmore, Whirlpool, Maytag,
who needs Norge, Wards, Westinghouse, GE?

When I strung my clothesline from the post
where the rosebush fans over the redwood fence,
I was careful not to scare the rabbit away,
come to the yard for clover,
crouching on the cool ground along the fence
among the mint that's grown high as my knee;
it sits in there still and breathless with revelation,
the laundry like sweet apparitions flapping overhead,
my presence humming through the intoxicating leaves.
I wish that kind of myth to give my daughters,
as free of cruelty and lies
as the vision of this small waiting animal.
Today I have only this day so perfect for the wash
drying by sun and wind, and a miracle for the rabbit
at peace under the rose bush.

Whose Children Are These?

I

Whose children are these?
Who do these children belong to?
With no power to watch over,
He looks at them, sleeping,
Exhaustion overwhelming hunger,
Barely protected with burlap from the cold
Cabin. Fear and rage make him tremble
For them; for himself, shame that he can do no more
Than die for them,
For no certain purpose. He heard about the woman,
Margaret Garner, in spite of the white folks' silence.
How she killed two of hers
To keep them from being taken back;
killed herself after the others were taken back
Anyway. So she saved
Two. He couldn't save his Ellen and Henry.
Who do these belong to?
He doesn't dare kiss them
Now, but stands dreaming,
Willing these five back
To a place or forward to a time
He can't remember or imagine.
All he can do is find the place
He knows about. Leave now
Before dawn sets the white fields raging
And murders the North Star.

II

Grandsire, I kissed, blessed, chewed, and swallowed your rage
when I stood over the five you sent, warm in their beds,
and force-fed my stunned dumb soul to believe someone
owned, someone bought, someone sold at will
our children, Grandsire, I held them, I held them
as you could not, and revered that fierce mother
whose courage and whose solution I could not.
But we have not rescued them altogether;
we moved them through one dimension, from one killing
field to another on history's flat page,
1850s' slavery to 1980s' racism and murder.
Baraka has told us "They have made
this star unsafe, and this age, primitive,"
and it is so. I have stood over each child sleeping
and looked at each child and wanted to know
who decides to break our hearts one by one by one.
The Greeks named it Tyche and made a goddess of chance.
Here they call it this god's mysterious Will.
I have the children, but we have not saved them
from this primitive star, and I am unable to forgive.

10 September 1985

Special Bus

There's a bus, children with slack faces
in the next lane, on a field trip,
A sight to make a parent weep.
My culture and learning spreadeagle me
between what I feel and what I think I know,
force me to wonder why I've been five times
blessed or missed by chance
and others not:
Dennis, Jerry, Josh, Shani, Dara—
twenty-three years from birth to birth,
risk increasing with each—
I'm about to beg the light to change,
or give in to what I don't believe I know.
A child turns and looks at me
with a light that can't be there.
Please don't thank God
or my mom and dad will be forced to blaspheme
for my life.
The light changes.
The light dies.

Strangers Like Us: Pittsburgh, Raleigh, 1945–1985

The sounds our parents heard echoing over
housetops while listening to evening radios
were the uninterrupted cries running and cycling
we sent through the streets and yards, where spring summer
fall we were entrusted to the night, boys
and girls together, to send us home for bath
and bed after the dark had drifted down and eased
contests between pitcher and batter, hider and seeker.

Our own children live imprisoned in light.
They are cycloned into our yards and hearts,
whose gates flutter shut on unfamiliar smiles.
At the rumor of a moon, we call them in
before the monsters who hunt, who hurt, who haunt
us, rise up from our own dim streets.

Haunted House

1.

The smallest bones in Helen's body
Don't dampen amplitudes as they should,
And, deep inside, her ears hurt. Her drums
Are set at such exquisite tension against my music
That a few measures from a sonata
Or a lyric I thought I'd forgot
Invites someone I loved or wanted
Forty years ago to take me back, away,
While she is distracted by threshold pain,
And makes the house tremble with her complaint
Against the noise,
However quietly my deference plays for her.

2.

I've memorized dozens of songs, old
Now, and must be the last man alive
Who remembers the Four Tunes
And Savannah Churchill, and knows the words
To "Is It Too Late?" and "I Understand,"
At thirteen the first record I bought.
I thought my voice was good enough,
But girls wondered "Who is this strange
Boy singing to me?" They were charmed
But found it uncomfortable

And too odd to risk.
I married the first woman who didn't think so,
Who steered me arm in arm
Singing down dark streets
"The Nearness of You," who tried with me
My weird pastime of reading through
Ellington and Verdi scores.
But divorced and died away from that music,
I brought my life away on reels of taped 78s.

   3.

I sing to no one in this house,
Except alone, except to ghosts.
At the piano or stereo I cram
Eighth notes into my mouth with both
Hands, delight in the bite of their comet
Tails; sprinkle black pepper Thirty-
Seconds on my grits, crunchy crouton
Sixteenths on salads, make perfect Martinis
With black olive Quarter notes;
The powerful head-clearing Half note mints
Like the days of creation, prepare me
For the Whole, the cosmic egg,
The singular state of Nommo,
And I don't know that I'm not seeing
 Blue Whales swim among the Pleiades when Rachmaninoff
And Ray Charles are transformed to pressure waves
In the liquid Tympani of my inner ear;
When Callas sings, Segovia plays, or Divine Sarah
Divines, I can't swear that I don't hear
The fifty thousand hair cells
Rippling in my organs of Corti as I follow

The electric impulses
Along the thirty thousand fibers of my auditory nerve,
And the brain quadrupling that in numbers of stars
That light folk to goon on galactic pilgrimages
To empty tombs, stones newly rolled away.
And everywhere throughout Andromeda
Young men in castle windows weep
For our loss, for Helen's noise, for Helen's pain.

Yardwork

I

These leaves blow here from others' trees: it's spite
That makes me not rake them till spring. This year
I choose Good Saturday as my first day
In the yard, and find under mine the reason
My neighbors don't let their leaves
Lie all winter. I was straddling the pile,
Pulling toward me, when I heard the squeak.
I who had to ask my neighbor the names
Of crepe myrtle and ligustrum don't know this
Gunmetal blue creature crawling a bewildered circle
At my feet. A little white mixed in, round ears,
My mind insists "rabbit" to stop the reflex
Whose ignorance doesn't know a vole from a rat.
There are rabbits about, who eat the clover
When I don't cut grass often as Helen likes.
And last year I was forced to surrender to the one
I called Br'er, or Sis, the row of broccoli
And collards I tried to grow at the back door.
Even so, I hope it's not one of their chillun
I've raked or stepped on.
                            It's going
In circles, I think, because it's hurt. It drags
A leg. There's blood on its hindquarters. I don't
Bend down to diagnose, I stand straight
As the rake I hold. Oh God there's a hole in the ground

Packed with fur, moiling with blue motion. The creature
Takes on stature as a mother, or largest
In a litter. And I'm not any kind of healer.
As a child
The saintly John Woolman saw
A robin sitting in her nest. As he came
Near, she went off, but flew
About "with many cries," concerned
For her young. The boy threw stones
And killed her. Pleased at first, then seized
With horror, he climbed the tree and killed
The birds, supposing that better
Than leaving them to pine away
And die miserably. Tender mercies.
    At ten-thirty on a breezy morning the sun
Is mild, but there are no leaves now to filter
This light. I see those dark motions and comfort
Myself with a pathetic fallacy:
The one thing I can do is save them from
The cruel sun.
              Except for a careful mound
Near the fence, my putting back, the yard is cut
And raked. And under that mix of sycamore and fur,
Life goes on as it will.

II

              My daughters stand
On the bank and watch me free the creek. The water
Is usually clear, but people on Cooper Road
Use the street drain for whatever they choose: beer cans,
Broken toys, plastic and paper, old oil
That killed most of the crayfish that filled the stream

When it ran full from Taylor's Pond. Boys swam there
In spite of all he could say or do.
Who could blame him for breaking the dam? His drain
Pipe gave our back lots the diversions
Of running water. I built my own small dam
To amplify the sound, and watched the crayfish
Swim, clean, cleanly.
                       The girls want to see
What's under the leaves. Like me, they would prefer
Rabbits to mice. But I want nothing disturbed.

I've never seen that shade of living blue.
If that was the mother circling in the sun—
Well, Woolman didn't say how he did it.
I have gasoline. To pour and stifle. Or to burn.

I've raked a turtle shell heavy with mud
Onto my side of the creek. I can't tell the girls
If it's alive, but they lean over to watch
A lone, "dungy" crayfish struggle out of
The cloud I've stirred up. I roll the shell,
Alive or dead, back into the slow stream.

It won't be there tomorrow.
                             Tomorrow the eggs
I hide for my daughters in the yard
Will be large plastic pantyhose
Containers, filled with foil-wrapped
Chocolates. Nothing to do with bunnies,
No "real" eggs that raise the dead.
But under the russet leaves, life
Will go on as it will. Or it will not.

What More?

My lawnmower has awakened the resident god of my yard
who rubs its leafy hand in anticipation
of troubling me again with one of its cruel koans,

this one a small bird dropped
from the sky, or thrown out,
out of the sweetgum tree

where I was cutting
that long triangle of grass outside
the back fence: put there

when I wasn't looking, it lies
on its back twitching half in and out of the swath
I cut a minute before.

I'm being tampered with again,
like an electron whose orbit and momentum
are displaced by the scientist's measurement

and observation. If I'd found something already stiff
and cold on the ground
I'd have kicked or nudged it out of my path:

but the just-dead, the thing still warm,
just taken its last breath, made its last
movement, has its own kind of horror.

I leave the small patch of uncut grass around it.
Back inside my enclosed yard
I see a brown thrasher come and stand over the body,

with some kind of food in its bill.
(I was careful to say "bill" and not "mouth.")
By the next time I cut myself around the yard,

I see the thrasher sitting on the fence above the still dead,
still holding whatever it has in its bill. I've described
it all accurately. What more could anyone expect of me?

Plot

I'm not certain
                yet
I don't believe I'll attend
her grave or stone
because there will be nothing here to see.
These flowers are for the living,
but not for me; I'd have bluejays screaming for her:
I was always birdboy, and she is flowergirl.
No. I'll stay at home
and cry in our bed alone
where I can remember
                    even now
we are dying of loneliness

in each other's arms.

Theology

Driving five-year-old Dara to school December 15,
she tells me that God was visible
when he created the world,
but that made him tired,
so he died,
and went to heaven,
then he became invisible.

Suddenly *I* understand Lao-Tzu, Plato,
Augustine and Aquinas,
Barth, Tillich,
all those guys—

the whole thing.

Epigraphs

1.

> *Melville B. Cox*
> *—1799–1833—*
> *Minister of Edenton St.*
> *Methodist Church, 1831.*
> *First American Methodist*
> *Missionary to Africa, 1833.*
> *"Let a thousand fall before*
> *Africa be given up."*
>
> Historical marker, Raleigh, N.C.

The man and his dates obsess me. Each day
I go to work or take my daughter to school
And pass his memorial I curse and swear,
Shake my head, or smile knowingly. This is all
I want to know about him, though he seduces
Me with motives, taxes my imagination
With scenarios of his death. Whose Africa
To give up, or keep for whose benefit?
Thousands fell to temptation, shook African
Trees, and black fruit fell into their salvation
Sacks, into the holds of their ships. Think of it:
An American missionary of that Peculiar
Institution in that place! With some
Humility he might have been British,
Who abolish slavery in their Empire;

That year: Johannes Brahms and Alfred Nobel
Are born, Edmund Keane dies, Santa Anna
Is President of Mexico, Oberlin
College is established, Tennyson begins
In Memoriam, the American Anti-
Slavery Society is founded, Melville B. Cox
Dies in Africa. I hear him howling with bloody
Flux, see his innocent arrogance enrage
The gods there who drive him mad, or become a Host
For his intended converts. I don't need "facts"
To affirm the truth of this dark allegory.
He would've been better advised to stay home,
Read the papers and notices for slave
Sales, observe and preach to his neighbors, and devote
His nights and days to theodicy.

2.

Much Madness is divinest Sense—
To a discerning Eye—

                Emily Dickinson

I envy you, Mr. Blake,
set screaming at four
when God looked in through your window,
and never a moment's doubt.
I believe in belief
that drives one mad,
when the darkroom door
swings open onto a nova that burns all the images
to blank white   freeze dried naked   and you hear
the uniform hiss of background noise in space

roaring in your mouth—profound terror
after the fact
and not the prudent wager,
and not ashamed to say
Yes that looks like God out there to me
and yes there are angels in that tree
and yes I see the ghost of that flea.
    If you are mad, Mr. Blake,
it's not the poet in you: the sanest of men:
what God sends poets with rifles and missions
to the tops of towers, to shopping centers, holy wars?
What poets go?
Heaven isn't that far away.
    At fifty-four I can still scream, Mr. Blake,
though I've already seen in the eye of a Humpback whale
the doomed tolerance of your face at the window.
But I'm nearly as willing to let my mind go a little,
to lean against the sun,
for one more poem.

3.

> "The vices of mankind are active and able ministers of depopulation. They are the precursors in the great army of destruction; and often finish the dreadful work themselves."
>
>   Thomas Malthus, *An Essay on*
>   *the Principle of Population*

Earth is not supporting us, we are dying
Of malnutrition, starving by millions,
Not doing enough to check populations.

We are failing as Protestants and Catholics, Jews,
Sunni and Shiite Muslims, Hindus and Sikhs.
We need more and more Faith, more Religions.
Or soccer would suffice, with daily world-
Wide championships in Brazil and Brussels.

For the survivors, let them thank the god
Who wins that animals have no known worship,
Or sports, and there will be food enough for man
At last, for the worst that some animals do
(who kill their kind only to eat)
Is to kill their food by eating it.

4.

> *"This was not the work of God—it was the work of Satan."*
>
> A mother who survived a tornado in Albion,
> Pennsylvania, June 1985. Eighty-six dead.

But he once was Lucifer, outwitted from that proximate height,
From one abstraction to a lesser, stripped
And streaming gorgeous photons of morning light
Like an electron descending levels of energy
And belief to rest in the mind's underkingdom
Until aroused by her despair: she shifts him
From one hemisphere to the other, reassigning
Power, endowing him with God's jealous sovereignty
To make the horror bearable. And who
Is he to question the theology of grief?
And how will she sleep nights now that she

Has transformed her enemy's will into *tornado*,
Reshaping with its twisted foot her wild
Heart into an altar's sacrifice for her child?

5.

*"I knew God meant for me to win this one of these
days. He didn't let me down."*
Reba McEntire, upon being
voted Female Vocalist of the Year at the
Country Music Association Awards, 1985

Now we lay us down to dream,
Things are better than they seem,
And every dog will have its day.
Pray and wait just long enough,
Being faithful, hanging tough,
He'll serve us what we order, "all the way."

Bumper signs say "PRAYER WORKS"
And some who pray are clearly jerks
To make Him trivialize that terrible power.
Not even taking His name in vain,
Coaches pray to win the game,
And expect results within the hour.

Take Him now, for all He's worth,
Taking is our right by birth,
Adam won it with his fall.
Now we lay us down to dream,
Keep it little, keep it mean;
We've made Him in our image, after all.

Greyhound

In the Post Houses
I obsessively, compulsively flush
Rows & rows of golden urinals.

Polar's TV Fantasy

It's a queer bear that doesn't like history.
Polar dreamed his own:
The columned white house, the lazy drive

Heavy with trees, the little quaint homes
Near the fields, wenches always, willing,
The happy happy people.

Poor Polar Wife *was* a queer bear
Who didn't like the history she saw being made
From behind the curtains of their dream house:

Faces like her children's faces, sons, daughters,
In the fields, serving in the house,
Everywhere.
She wasn't quite that kind of ideal fool.
She resented the risk, but was forced
To look into the fire
Of Polar history: a call to obedience,

A stone mountain, a stone knife.
Of one accord they acknowledged
But ignored the progeny in the fields,

Serving in the house,
Everywhere,
And sold whom they pleased.

Now they please, and congratulate themselves
With the Polar TV national
Fantasy, buying back and adopting

Black males! black males!
Into their families, cute, irresistible cheeks, but males
Nevertheless forbidden, doomed never to become men among
    them.

Sportsfan

Its appearance is human.
And so it may be.

Certainly it exhibits humanlike feelings
in its doglike devotion and loyalty
to the jockspecies on which it exists in symbiosis.
Its lifecycle is seasonal,
during which and according to the fortunes
of its team it becomes dangerous—
murderous, suicidal, destructive of property
private and public.
Its herd instinct is deceptively passive,
displaying aggressive group behavior
at those sportingevents that sustain it,
give it identity and sense of self
and where its actions
and forms of communication
are embarrassing to human parents
and unsuitable for small children.
Its sexual activity
is also seasonally influenced,
interest and energy dissipated
or drained off through TV tubes.
Exceptions may occur
during Homecoming and Championship rituals
when it has been known to engage in genital display
and public copulation.

However, only a bigot
would insist that all
are ugly and loud,
barbaric and boorish
because of the majority.
They may be
some of your best friends
who never act in any way
that arouses suspicion.
It depends on the season.

But it is perfectly understandable
that you would not want
your daughter
or your son
to marry one.

War Film: Dying Forever

In my living room forty-four years later
the marine is running and wading
off the landing barge into the water,
onto the beach at Tarawa.
It must've been blue, it must've been loud,
Hellcats and Corsairs from the carrier going in,
mortar, small arms, battleships firing into the island,
machine guns chattering its name.
The tall strange trees ahead must've surprised him
for a moment,
it could've been beautiful, the surf,
all that sun and those trees, the feathery tops,
if the word exotic was known
to a steelworker from Pennsylvania,
if there was time enough,
running toward the sand
on *The Twentieth Century* with Walter Cronkite.
It's all black and white to me
from the photographer's perspective
who must've been one of the first on the beach,
then turned his back to the land
to film what was coming in from the sea.
And there, there is the exact moment, without firing a shot,
our Marine Harry Allmon from Homestead is hit by a round
    or more
from the Japanese soldier neither he nor I
will ever see,

and the moment he falls forward, pack, rifle, helmet,
the moment he stumbles in the water off Tarawa 1943
he is dead.
In war films on either side
I've seen the already dead,
like twentieth-century bodies,
stacked cordwood,
or rolling in surf, dead already forever.
But in this moving picture
this fall of this single man
traps me in his surprised sorrow.
Like the savior he would be
of ourselves
from all battles
who dies on demand for instant replay,
the technologies of war and film
keep him dying forever,
forever.

Uniforms

> "*Again we say, of the North as of the South, that life for us is daily warfare and that we live hard, like soldiers . . . . the color of our skins constitutes our uniforms . . .*"
> Richard Wright, *12 Million Black Voices (1941)*

They have never died in our uniforms
as we have in theirs.
It was easier to die in battle,
in the uniform of United States Colored Troops,
than on the plantations,
easier even at Fort Wagner, or Fort Pillow
when the gray demons shot and burned us
in our blue, prisoners of war.
We didn't want to die, but did.
All we ever wanted was to be free.
We died for that freedom, and theirs, too,
at Verdun, in the Argonne Forest,
and came back to familiar Chicago, Knoxville, Omaha
where they lynched us in khaki,
dishonored their own uniforms,
made a nightmare of their dream.
We didn't want to die at the Bulge,
at the Rhine and Arno Rivers,
on Pork Chop Hill, at Danang and Hue,
but we did,

becoming less sure whose freedom we were dying for.
For still, in places with familiar names
hooded men shame their faith as Christian Knights
of burning crosses,
enhance with sheets the color of the faces
that we often would die not to see, for just one day.

He didn't want to die in Memphis,
not because of a dream
not even for a dream,
but he did, in uniform,
in daily warfare,
and free, free of hate, because all he ever wanted
was that they could be as free as we are.

For Martin Luther King, Jr.
18 January 1986

Where It Came From

Running shuttle buses in heaven would
not be right, would it? But if they do, I'll bet
they put TJ in a Caddy to feel at home.
But what kind of heaven would make me choose
between lover and husband just because someone
says "You are married, you are not"? Well, we
are not Ark animals to be herded to heaven by twos.
If heaven is free of sin, love will get us in.

So I'll have Earl there with Malcolm and me;
he'll be with me, his first wife Betty, and their kids.
I tell you, he adored that woman once.
And TJ won't have to hustle back and forth
between Margaret and me. Don't you think
that's only fair? TJ used to say
he could reason with a god who made mountains.
I believed in one who made strawberries,
and orgasms, too, and the man who gave me both,
in and out of season.
                        Oh—I'm sorry. That table
has a wobbly leg. Let me fill your glass.
We had more than common compatibility.
He was a womanly man, a woman's man,
he loved me in the way a woman would.
You know what I mean, you, a woman too.
He needed me to let him be that way.
Margaret, though, she wouldn't. Well, she *couldn't*.

She's the one, you see, needed a stud.
But I found places on him how they say
men are supposed to do for *us*, with mouth
and hands, and made his body bloom like mine.
He never was foolish enough to claim
his woman wasn't good to him. I know
they both were trapped in roles they played for each other.
He told me. It was like a wrestling match,
each mind trying to get back
into the body it needed, each trying to show
the other how to use the body it had.
Except for that, they needed each other.
They belonged to those Alphas or Deltas
or some such, I never could remember.
They put those his and hers bumper stickers
on that absurd car he bought. I know her.
I'm glad he told you about us, you understand,
he couldn't have talked to anyone else.
TJ's brother, that pious prick, doted
on him; he would've been outraged that baby
brother, the model husband, had a whore
on the side. I know why TJ asked you
to come, you still almost a stranger, his absent
daddy's daughter. I know you. He let me
see you first time you came, his newfound sister.
He had to tell someone about the letters.

We met at a convention, in a session
where he was talking on marketing demographics.
I liked him, right then, on the spot.
I thought what a cute little dude—if only he had
some hair on his face. We talked the rest of the night.
I did, about Earl, for hours, our heads almost touching.

I'd never let anyone in me—mother, sister,
husband, yet here this man I'd never see again
sat listening to me talk.
If we had touched, I might have done anything.
Everything. I don't know where it came from.
It was like a dream counterfeiting memory.
I was astonished again months later
when I got his letter. What I can't
bear about this is, I couldn't see him,
I couldn't say goodbye. Oh. Oh God
it must've been bad—you say the casket was closed.
I went to that memorial service they had
at that snooty church he sometimes attended.
I listened to that drivel, knowing TJ
would rather be in my arms, or Margaret's,
than at *His* Everlasting Bosom.
Snooty? What? Yes. He started going there
after he and Margaret moved to Lochmere Highlands,
and joined that Black Country Club,
that bunch of snots, and bought that damned car.
One thing I don't know, was afraid to ask,
whose idea that was, who wanted it.
I always suspected he probably watched
"Lives of the Rich and Famous," or some such crap.
But TJ was my best friend, and in a lover
there are things you don't have to deal with.
No one else called him that but me.
I hated TyRONE almost as bad as LEEroy.
If he'd been born a generation before,
who knows? Rufus. Rastus. Rufus Rastus
Johnston Brown. But we don't name ourselves,
do we? Like those kids of his and Margaret's,
the latest trend. La Toyadonya something,

and Otoyota, is that it?
                    I guess I'm kidding.
I knew when they were born. I went and saw them
through the window. I prayed for them later
when they were sick. We were like all family.
But only TJ and me knew.
If Earl had known how much in this house is here
because of TJ! This room we're sitting in,
this room? Mostly TJ's. When we did over
the house I asked his advice, his sense of things,
color, balance, proportion, all that,
that I don't have a bit of. He even
did old Earl's study. The leather, prints,
the recessed bookshelves?—all his ideas. You know
Earl left me? He finally figured out
there was somebody, but didn't know who.
I wouldn't ever tell. I said no
when TJ came and said he'd leave Margaret
if I'd marry him. He claimed I saved his marriage.
Then said he'd leave her! Ain't that a wonder.
He thought I said no to save it again.
The man just did not understand.
Looking back, I know when I should've seen it.
You know when he had that little Chevy?
We used it once to go see a client
because the company car broke down.
Came back through one of those neighborhoods,
like the one they later moved into,
because he wanted to gawk at all the *homes*.
I wanted to slide and hide in my seat,
but Lord you know I kept my mouth shut.
Easy to do when you a side woman.
But I found reasons not to ride in that—

that other car.
A long time ago, that was in Cleveland,
I used to see the pimps, and—do you know Tolson?
I read *Harlem Gallery* to keep up with Earl—
The pimps and "Cadillac Philistines," cruising,
some without a pot to piss in. I swore
I'd not get in one if it wasn't my hearse.
That was the only time he disappointed me.
He was so smug that day, and my heart sank
when I saw it. It's a nice color I said.
My head must still be living in the sixties
when we marched and tried to change the symbols
that defined us. But he made me wonder
was it worth my busted head freeing slaves to play golf.
Our ladies of color are frying their hair again.
Our men have become Medusas of greasy curls.
My hair? I know. The natural is dated now,
a kind of symbol, too. But he said he liked it,
liked the novelty of knowing a woman
who didn't go to the beauty parlor every week.
Though TJ stayed in the barbershop enough
for him and Maggie both. Anyway,
a lover is a lover, a friend is a friend.
A husband is something else. I wouldn't marry him, though,
good to me as he was. He made me laugh.
What kind of man can break you up
with laughter, making love, and keep passion going?
I don't know where it came from.
He did impressions, and he was good, too.
You couldn't imagine some of the men
I've been to bed with. Think what it would be,
having Laurel and Hardy and Eddie Murphy
all on top of you at the same time!

He was that kinda sweet man. I loved him.
He knew I did. And he knew I loved Earl, too.
TJ was why I didn't leave that bastard.
I caught him with a grad student, once,
that little bitch, right there in that study.
He was lucky I didn't turn his ass in,
get him kicked out. But TJ said,
"Joanna, maybe he loves the girl, or needs her."
I was speechless. Lord, I wanted to kick
his little ass, too. But he knew how much
I loved Earl and how Earl needed me.
He was that kind of sweet man
and I loved him, I do. But I wouldn't ride
with him in that vulgar Negro car.

Wonder what Margaret's gonna do with it now?
She never worked, never learned to drive,
just sat on her fat ass all day,
sitting and sitting on her family's money,
except when she had poor TJ
drive her around like a chauffeur to her clubs.
What's she gonna do now? What will she do?
I've got a thing or two to tell that . . .

Thank you for the letters. These are all he had?
Yes, he wouldn't have kept the rest. Must you rush away?
Of course. I do thank you. My son Malcolm
will be home soon—so much like his dad—
I know you'd like him, you would. I do wish
you two could meet before you go back to Phoenix.

Optimum Distance

You stop at my door, see my eyes touch you
And feel our memory waken your dark nipples,
Sleeping now under the summer dress. I hold
A question for you in the air, and hear how
The gesture recalls my hand poised over the dish
At Peng's when you laughed at the likeness you saw
Between the glazed brown mushrooms and me.
The doors we stand in now are public exits
To lunch and spa, no more passage ways
Into rooms we made for lovers, whose presence we hide
In public countenance, like facing mirrors
We are ourselves confused by the risky friendship
Of incomparable love. Neither divorced,
Discovered, nor unfaithful, we moved without

Imperative, restrained only by will,
Into this nine-to-five zone of middle dimensions,
Imprisoned by everyday physics
In the illusion of solid bodies and empty space.
Sometimes I wish us back to letter distance,
When arranged meetings were rare enough to number.
We carefully risked the unexpected savage
Storm, broken fan belt, dead battery,
Inexplicable call for help forty miles
Beyond the range of reasonable trust. Within
The radius of next day delivery,
We used to disappear into primal mornings

Or evenings, borrowed from anyone who wasn't
Paying attention, and change them back into time

So raw that we wept when we saw the whales walking
In ponderous adagio into their fatal dream of the sea.
The cloudforest canopy covered us
On our preferred floors in borrowed apartments
Sunlight, afternoons, through the potted ferns
Your lascivious lion licked its muzzle and watched
You raise your knees for me, I remember you
Imagining my "soft brown head" rising and setting
In your orbit, at your pleasure, before
The moon was born. "Vampire," someone says
Inadvertently in conversation and our skin
Feels the unpressed corduroy and flannel;
We loved across your bed, mostly clothed
In the cold, the night we saw *Nosferatu*.

Once an obsession took us on a mid
Night from one house sleeping to one house empty,
To lie naked, talking, sword between us.
Altogether mad, we stole three brilliant
Days in a dry November, like diamonds,
From whomever had left them carelessly about.
We drove them across two states, let them hear
What Miles Davis's *Concierto* sounded like
Fifty-six floors above the Mississippi,
In nothing less than unrimed first moonlight.
In our own light we changed rooms into cloud
Chambers, like particles in furious collision,
Energy creating matter like itself, ourselves, we
Split, divided love again and love again,

    Identical each time, and whole.
                                We leave cloud
Tracks all over town for the lovers who haunt
Us to have their bodies back.
                            The beached whales
You saw last October had come to call
Us back from city parks and potted forests.
In our masks of decorum we keep such difficult balance
In company, with such casual care
(back with such odd secrets of the line to tell).
No one imagines that we might be the first
Lovers of the world, who made possible the world
They know. Listen. The lovesick lion who mumbled
At your hands is not in the zoo. Come away.
Look. The whales are coming back to land, re-
Versing everything. Friend, this is too risky. Let's go back.

Universe

On a day like this
I can forget the universe expanding in all directions;
here your hand strokes away
strokes the anxiety
of not knowing whether it will go on stretching
into cold gossamer as stars die out
or snap back into our faces with another bang.
We are at risk out there
where every atom in us
originated when the large stars exploded;
all our elements will drift
back into space
when the sun dies, however it goes.
But here
here by chance and necessity
we can trust the wisdom of our bodies
if nothing else, as old as the first explosion,
as alike as to our common ancestor,
the first cell struck by lightning or radiation
from which all life here evolved.

And we here by chance and necessity
developed in synchrony,
shaping ourselves to each other's needs
(this tongue never used this way before,
the size and shape of these breasts exactly right,
this finger, finding its place and sliding into that fold,

this hair abundant and crisp where it should be,
this waist and back perfect, deep, curved for the arms underneath)
Here, Love, is a new cheese for you to try,
rich, buttery, flavored with garlic and spices,
a wine from Ethiopia,
plums nearly as dark as your nipples,
all from the same cell that made us,
whose nucleic acids may be present in this room,
in one of us
in
in
wait. wait.
it's expanding again and
the explosion

Bill Two

Dear lady in Chicago
Or wherever you were then
(It's been a long time, I'm not sure)
Bill Sledd was no gentleman toward you
He was a dirty rat
He either lied about you or told the truth
He told us all about you and his baby
This was at Sampson Air Force Base in '53, basic training
So you'll know the right one
You were his high school teacher? Music?
Or was it your husband who taught him?
I almost had your name
Nina, Ingrid, who or what
What did you see in him we wondered
We looked at him and wanted to know
Before black was beautiful
That arrogant son of a bitch
With his freckles and sandycurly hair
He wasn't tall dark and handsome
If women like you liked that type
But how could we doubt him
That son of a bitch showed us the picture
I think it was the first Polaroid I'd seen
Unless it was developed by your husband
Your body burning bursting full and ripe in my eyes
Before the baby, I think,
Your hair cut short and across the forehead

Like Keely Smith's.
And the hair, the other growth, damn him!
The black perfect triangle above your thighs
Was the troubling center of the photo
I would've stolen if I could
So dense it has shaped my life to this day.
I almost had your name again
Laura? Wanda? I'd tell it if I knew.

I found you once or twice
But it wasn't the same.

Are you all right?
How is the baby?
Who does it look like?
I hope your husband doesn't find out
I hope he finds out and kicks Bill's ass
That son of a bitch told us horny airmen everything
I was nineteen and you have always been older than me
But that's all right.
My name is Bill too.
It will never be too late for me.

Adagio

That morning you found your lights on,
battery dead, came back to the apartment,
walked in wet and blinking rain at me,
and we went back to the narrow bed

where always I hear the short *Ah!*
when I enter you.
Twenty years, I'll never see you again.
Barber's *Adagio* came six years later.

It's what we wanted for those three months,
for the days I'm going to live with,
like the strings sinking, and sinking:

each time you come back I think
it will be the last time
and I won't know it,
like the last breath I don't remember taking.

Untitled

She caught a butterfly
and held it closed
   lightly
in her hand.
She released it
because the sensation made by its
   fluttering
wings was unpleasant.
When the butterfly let itself be caught
   again
she killed it.

Cello Poem

> "*I hear the violoncello, ('tis the young man's heart's complaint)*"
>
> Walt Whitman

I

Another guest room on the poetry circuit   dim and elegant   dark furniture   I drive the Hertzcar   looping and crisscrossing the state alone as salvation from deadly smalltalk   Gambier   Wooster   Oxford   New Concord   Athens   eight campuses in six days   I follow maps and directions sent ahead in strange hands

"Denise Levertov stayed here last year"   Well   What to say to that   "How did she like it?"?   "Did she sleep well?"?   "Were her dreams blessed or troubled by the presences of exhausted poets before her?"?

Yesterday a woman whom I will always love drove twenty seven miles to hear me read her poem   Afterwards we delayed outside at her car in an operatic November night so mild and unbearable I felt relief that our past would remain where we'd left it   She drove away ten years further back than she'd come   Alone in the heavy room   six years away from hometown neighbor Pittsburgh and unreachable from Raleigh   I remember Cincinnati's WLW and American Airlines' *Music in the Night* lights off hours after midnight except for the

glow when radios had tubes and were warm and
hummed at my bedside   I turn and find it   Everything
turns   I hear the violoncello

I couldn't have heard it before   never   I couldn't have
ever heard it in all the ugly duckling years when music
loved me only   When I became violin   piano   guitar
harmonica   When I chose as my favorite siblings
oboe   French and English horns   When the trained
sopranos   mezzos   tenors constricted my heart with
electricity and omnipotence   When I could have passed
out in the Westinghouse High School orchestra   for
joy   because I was in it   third chair   first violin: even
then   when the physical beauty of the thing had sung to
my eyes   I hadn't heard it   Fascinated   I'd see around
my music stand the girls holding the cello between their
wide-skirted legs   Its sound in their hands was
nasal   whining   but my dumb soul was dazzled by its
posture enshrined where it was

My first mature love at eighteen   with the longest legs
I'd ever seen   called a boy's name   had played cello in
school before we met   I never heard her   but could
always see her doing it   When those legs were
mine   they were the least of what we both wanted   not
for want of trying   Smart college kids   we knew what
we were supposed to know and kissed and kissed it all
without experience   our bodies denied us full use   shut
against us   we kissed away the difficulty we declared
marriage would give us time to solve: kissed standing
and lying   bodies grinding with such ferocity I'd ride
midnight streetcars home still engorged   groin aching
from her sharp pubic arch   a miracle we didn't become

nearly virgin parents on those winter evenings she
slouched to the edge of the chair before me   her wide
skirt at ease to be kissed   her endless legs molding me
into the shape of her cello

The bed gleams maple like her cello body in the dim room
sounding me   I hear Dvorak's concerto   in the allegro the
cello's sixteenth notes rippling under the flute and oboe
melody in and through me in twenty-five measures   and gone
before I can recover
       before I can recover I hear
            the cello's revelation:
                 its rich androgynous sound
is the voice of single trees
not those conventional horns for massed forest
or the string tremolos and slow trills for leaves and wind
             before I can recover I'm deafened
       by the secret   trees of the virgin rain forests
    celloing in the earth's holy lands
around the green belt of Zaire   Brazil   Gabon   Indonesia
before I can recover I hear a choir of cellos
war cry cello of the Zulu warrior
   kidnapped cry of the Yoruba father
      Comanche cello whose bow and strings
          sing brief victory
dirty blues cello of a good woman done wrong
young French Chinese virtuoso cellist of Bach and jazz
dozens of women cellists who overcame mothers' doubts
of its unladylike demands   lovely   like woman and horse
aesthetic   sensual in their affinities
Spanish and Russian cellos of the old interpreters
               Kali cello of the slipping strings
           Charli's cello   first mature love

      between whose knees I wove a timespace mobius
to keep me each moment
where I would be
in this room alone:
          I see it all:
      she played the cello   she loved me
   I left that music back with her   but around the mobius
strip again we reverse positions   cello between my knees
playing
like the old men Casals   Rostropovich   Starker   this time
I choose interpretation and wisdom over virtuosity
     Alone I have no one to tell what I hear and see
        how stunned I am with its fullness
            my only despair that
I have no one to tell: not Helen at home whose ears hurt
to the noise she hears   I'd had to let go the siblings
whom music   who loved me   sent as lovers.
Before I can recover, it is morning.

II

Through the window at the kitchen sink,
I see white dogwood blaze across the grass.
I wash morning dishes, contentedly blank,
Until I hear the music, Gounod's *Mass*
For St. Cecilia, on the radio
Reminding me of Easter. I can't breathe
Against those voices, whose words I don't know,
Or with loved ones in church praying away death.
Praying my world away. I see the white explosion
Dim, the oak and pine waver and fade
From the force of that dreamy congregation.

I take my cello to the woods to serenade
The trees in their own voice, and repay
Them a soul to survive that judgment day.

III

Before we know how much we can presume
Upon the perfect pitch of compatibility,
We play to make time stand still in the room.

In our adagio ease, slow duets bloom
In afternoons that beggar hyperbole
Until we learn how little we can presume.

A nocturne together, a prize rare as a black plume:
Naked bodies tuned on the balcony over a moonlit sea
We play to make time stand still in the room.

Aubades on each other's instrument; perfume
Of honeysuckle through the window with tea,
Cheese, astonishment, and plums: we presume

Such excess as ours will bring certain doom,
Obsession in winter's fevered memory,
And pray time to stand still in the room.

Harmonics on touched nerves, like strings, a loom,
Weave delirium into epiphany.
Before we know better than to presume,
We have played time to a standstill in our room.

IV

My body can't use the logic of never
Having her again, can't credit the threat
That today and the next will be the same forever.

I torment and solace my soul with the quaver
Of my cello's lowest, most poignant string; yet
The body will hear no reason she is never

There when it thrusts against its own fever.
I can't explain to it *regret*
That this season could be the same forever.

How the wind blows in across the river.
Now our clandestine park's turned dark and wet.
What she left is immune to metaphor, may never

Sing or roar again if not to survive her:
Love imprisons me in her debt
In a year that might be the same forever.

My solo hands surge toward her absence, maneuver
My obsession to fake the chords of an old duet.
The body will hear no reason. Never.
This life and the next may be the same forever.

V

Whitman, who "broke the new wood," showed me
Where to find the trees.
The cello top is soft, resonant tone-wood

From a high stand of Engelmann spruce in Oregon,
Slow to mature in loamy soil, winged seeds, pendent cones;
For neck, sides, and back, the dense Big-leaf maple,
Exotic in appearance when finished.
To make my own instrument I had to subdue
The living, rebellious wood with art, craft, and science,
Carving across its grain to form the arching, the swell
Of the cello top, whose shaping determines the instrument's
Ultimate sound.
And a "manual laborer," as Casals called himself,
Who, like the slow spruce, cared not a whit for time,
Devoting a year to learning a Bach suite,
Who showed me that age alone may not improve
The instrument, but will get better if played well.
Holding it between the knees, I surround it
With my own, can hear and feel that belltoned wood still
Breathing into me body to body, neck, ribs, belly, back,
Hair of the bow, grip, nut, adjusting screw,
Playing what I've made from trees, consonants, vowels,
In my own forest, on an unfretted instrument without stops
And guides, I learn the string player's habit of hearing tones
Mentally before playing them,
Playing often at the edge of an abyss of error
And worse, ignorance. But my own, free, my own.

VI

I've mastered the cello for this: to fester
With music, with praise I've found no One to give.
I transcribe and play the gorgeous myths,
A pyramid for a Plumed Serpent, sacrificial
Cauldrons worked in silver, a *Pieta, Apollo,*

A Glorious mosque with exquisite *mihrabs* at Cordoba,
Masterpieces of *Adoration* in centuries of canvas;
I practice *Requiems* and *Passions* in dumb reverence.

Yet in them lurk the Sun and Humming Bird,
Gods whose teeth ache for beating hearts;
Who are not shamed by Inquisition, Middle
Passage, Holocaust; who bless the Faithful
With the duty of war, with reward of death and Heaven.
Who leave the soloist with only his art to avert disaster.

VII

For years I didn't know she disliked the part
I'd assigned her. She played it so well, I'd swear
Her passion was all for love, and nothing of art.

Nevertheless, there was that contralto affair.
It was so undeserved, so unbecoming,
She swore, "No more," and then took up the snare.

She'd done her best all ways to please me, humming
The romantic arrangements, never in her key,
And too slow for the tempo of her drumming.

What she prizes is dispatch and brevity,
And wants no playing before we start to play.
My cello needs skillful tuning, but she

Demurs, tone deaf to my C, G, D, and A,
Leaving me to tune my own, not knowing
What close harmonies she sends marching away

TatataDUM tatataDUM I can't keep up, slowing
Her down, retarding her pace, denying her rare
Finales with my vain cadenzas and showy bowing.

We play in adjacent, nervous spaces, a pair
Of soloists of virtuoso *ad libitum*,
Whose clashing rhythms reduce us to despair.

Her crisp, insistent flam and drag beats numb
My stuttering fingers. My arrogance now undone,
I surrender to the taDUM ta DUM taDUM DUM DUM

That underscores whatever grace we've won.
Any music at all is better than none.

A former Woodrow Wilson Fellowship Visiting Author and Ford Foundation graduate fellow as well as the recipient of the 1983 Callaloo Creative Writing Award for Nonfiction Prose, Gerald Barrax is an associate professor of English at North Carolina State University and the editor of *Obsidian II*.